On March 23, 2010, President Barack Obama set in motion the radical remaking of America's health care system by signing the Patient Protection and Affordable Care Act into law. Three years later, the law's implementation is well under way. But to fully grasp what's ahead, we must take stock of what the law has already done, what Congress can do now, and what a future replacement agenda would look like.

Federal bureaucrats began implementing the 2,700-page law soon after President Obama put pen to paper. By 2013, they'd issued 20,000 pages of regulations. In August 2010, the Department of Health and Human Services (HHS) distributed $46 million in grants to assist states with what the administration dubbed insurance-rate reviews. Another $199 million flew from federal coffers for the same purpose in February 2011.

These "rate reviews" require insurers to publicly justify premium increases of 10 percent or more. In a majority of states, officials have the power to reject premium hikes they

deem unreasonable. At that point, rate reviews amount to price controls.

Starting in September 2010, all family policies were required to cover children up to age 26. Backers of the provision claimed that it would extend coverage to a demographic with one of the highest uninsured rates: young adults. But it's done so at their parents' expense, driving up premiums by $151, to $452 per year.

Obamacare tacked on three more cost-inflating mandates in 2010. The first mandate restricted insurance companies from placing lifetime limits or annual caps on the amount of coverage a customer could consume. From 2012 to 2014, no policy can cover less than $2 million in benefits annually, and in 2014, annual caps become illegal. The next mandate banned insurers from denying coverage to children with pre-existing conditions. The third prevented insurers from charging for anything that HHS categorized as preventive care. While popular, all three rules have made coverage less affordable.

In 2011, the feds began directly regulating insurers' profit margins with minimum medical loss ratios (MLRS). These rules require insurance companies to spend 80 percent of premiums from the individual and small-

---

Many doctors have seen enough of Obamacare. One 2012 survey found that a third of doctors plan to leave private practice in the next decade.

---

group markets and 85 percent of premiums in the large-group market on claims.

Insurers are having trouble meeting those standards. According to a February 2013 report by the Centers for Medicare and Medicaid Services, 24.5 percent of private insurers fell afoul of the MLR rules in at least one market in 2011. That same report estimated that insurers paid 13.1 million policyholders $1.1 billion in rebates for failing to meet those minimum medical loss ratios.

They'll look to avoid those rebates in the future. With most administrative costs fixed, the easiest way for insurers to comply is by raising premiums and simply paying health care providers more money. That's no way to make coverage more affordable – or address our nation's health-cost crisis.

Insurers haven't been alone in attracting Obamacare's ire. In September 2010, the feds began their assault on the pharmaceutical industry by creating the Patient-Centered Outcomes Research Institute (PCORI). This organization will oversee the administration's "comparative-effectiveness research" efforts – and will take its funding from a new fee on insurers. That fee started at $1 per beneficiary in 2012; each year thereafter through 2019, the fee runs $2 per beneficiary.

Comparative-effectiveness research purports to compare treatments against one another to determine which ones work best.

But those comparisons inevitably become biased by cost considerations. With health spending spiraling upward, PCORI will face substantial pressure to "discover" that older, cheaper remedies work just as well as newer, more expensive ones.

Defenders of PCORI claim that Obamacare forbids the agency from dictating coverage mandates or reimbursement levels. But that doesn't mean that private insurers or public payers like Medicare and Medicaid can't use the center's findings to adjust coverage and reimbursement decisions.

In 2012, the Obama administration lobbed a more direct volley at the pharmaceutical industry, extracting billions of dollars in new excise taxes calculated according to the previous year's sales volume. Obamacare collects these "fees" from the sector annually. Drugmakers will doubtless pass them along to consumers. Future generations will pay this tax, too, as it will divert money that would have been invested in the research and development of new cures to the federal Treasury instead.

Obamacare is also attempting to kill off the traditional private medical practice in favor of accountable care organizations (ACOs), which came into being in 2012. These networks of providers are supposed to coordinate Medicare patients' care – and thereby eliminate unnecessary or wasteful treatments. By the beginning of 2013, HHS announced that it had approved 106 new ACOs, bringing the nationwide total to more than 250.

ACOs force doctors and hospitals to assume significant financial risks and administrative burdens. Providers must absorb any losses they incur if they fail to realize the "savings" that regulators demand. They must also collect all sorts of data on health care quality. That data may be useful – but the infrastructure for obtaining it will cost billions. For all that extra spending, HHS expects to save $960 million from this arrangement over three years. That's less than 0.2 percent of what Medicare spends in one year, let alone three.

Many doctors have seen enough of Obamacare. One 2012 survey found that a third of doctors plan to leave private practice in the next decade. And a recent survey from Deloitte Consulting found that 70 percent of doctors are pessimistic about the future of their profession because of Obamacare. They have every right to be. After all, Obamacare's most disastrous provisions have not yet taken effect.

But they will over the next two years. What fresh nightmares can Americans look forward to?

2013

This marks the first year that many of Obamacare's onerous rules, regulations, and taxes take effect. But the law's signature insurance exchanges are commanding the attention of those charged with implementing it.

Insurance Exchange Uncertainty

Obamacare's authors made insurance exchanges – now rebranded as "marketplaces" – a central feature of their plan to expand access to health care, but their creation hasn't gone as smoothly as they had hoped. In April 2013, Senator Max Baucus (D-Mont.), the Senate Finance Committee chairman and one of the architects of the law, spoke with Kathleen Sebelius, the secretary of HHS, at a hearing on the exchanges. "I see a huge train wreck coming down," he said. He went on to say, "I'm very concerned that not enough is being done so far – very concerned." As part of the attempt to stave off this "train wreck," Sebelius has made many phone calls to foundations, companies, and community organizations – including many health-industry executives whose firms are affected by the law – asking for major donations to Enroll

Even with the promise of federal assistance, the cost to states of expanding the health care entitlement will be crippling.

America, the nonprofit group that supports expanding coverage in line with Obamacare's rules.

The exchanges are supposed to work like Internet shopping portals. The intention is to empower consumers who don't get coverage through work – as well as small businesses – to compare the costs and benefits of several health plans with the click of a button. The draft application form released by the administration in March was too complex and long. So in April, HHS released a shorter form that is touted to be much simpler. We shall see.

The exchanges are also to be the means by which the federal government distributes subsidies to help people purchase coverage. Starting in 2014, Americans with incomes between 138 percent and 400 percent of the federal poverty level – up to $94,200 for a family of four, as of 2013 – will qualify for federal health insurance aid. According to the Congressional Budget Office, some 26 million people will secure coverage through the exchanges in 2022.

Obamacare ordered the states to open their exchanges for enrollment by Oct. 1, 2013. Patients' coverage would then start on Jan. 1, 2014. But that schedule is looking unrealistic. Twenty-six states have refused to set up exchanges. Another seven declined to set them up on their own but agreed to partner with the federal government. Only 17 states and the District of Columbia said that they would create health insurance exchanges in accordance with Obamacare's dictates.

That leaves the federal government six months to set up exchanges for 26 states – and to assume a heavy operational and administrative load in seven more. Officials will have to vet insurers, hire and train staff, and create sophisticated and user-friendly new information-technology systems.

Obamacare's CO-OPs are among those waiting for the exchanges to take shape. Short for Consumer Operated and Oriented Plan, a CO-OP is a nonprofit health insurance provider owned and run by its members – which receives government assistance. CO-OPs will sell their plans on the insurance exchanges alongside other providers.

Federal aid to CO-OPs was trimmed from the original $6 billion allocated under Obamacare, but the federal government has already awarded nearly $2 billion in loans to help create new CO-OPs in 24 states. There's a danger that competition from these government-backed insurers will hurt private insurers, if not drive them out of some markets entirely.

That's bad news for consumers, who may face fewer insurance choices.

What Can Congress Do Now?

New taxes will offset about half the Affordable Care Act's cost, which was expected in 2010 to reach $944 billion over 10 years. By 2013, official estimates of its cost had swelled to $1.8 trillion through 2023. Republicans on the Senate Budget Committee put the total cost from 2014 to 2023 at $2.6 trillion.

With Obama's re-election and the Democrats keeping control of the Senate, what can be done now to reverse implementation of

Obamacare? Two things: repeal parts of the law and achieve positive results from court challenges.

Repeals

1. *Reverse Deductions for Medical Expenses.* For those with high medical bills, the most painful change will likely be the raising of the floor for deducting medical expenses on income-tax returns. Taxpayers used to be able to deduct medical expenses above 7.5 percent of their adjusted gross income. Now they can't take that deduction unless their medical expenses exceed 10 percent of their income. This shift could add hundreds of dollars to their tax bills – when they're least able to afford it.

2. *Reinstate Flexible-Spending Account Limits.* Obamacare halves the maximum annual contribution to a flexible-spending account (FSA), from $5,000 to $2,500. FSAs allow consumers to set aside funds pretax in order to pay for medical expenses. Many

FSA holders use the accounts to cover routine medical expenses like vision care, orthodontia, and prescription drugs.

Thanks to the tax hike, consumers may have to pay for such routine care with after-tax money – or shell out more for a comprehensive health insurance policy that covers these services. In either case, their wallets will be lighter.

3. *Reverse New Medicare Taxes.* 2013 marks the first year for $318 billion in new taxes on high earners – about half the tax revenue Obamacare is supposed to bring in over the next 10 years. Individuals who make more than $200,000 and couples earning more than $250,000 a year face a 0.9 percent surcharge on the 1.45 percent Medicare levy on earnings above those income thresholds. These earners will also have to pay a new tax of 3.8 percent on investment income.

The structure of these taxes penalizes married couples in particular. According to *The New York Times*, two singles who

A 2011 survey of 1,300 companies conducted by the consulting firm McKinsey found that almost a third planned to "definitely or probably" stop providing health coverage by 2014.

made $200,000 each would not owe any additional Medicare tax. But if they were married, they'd owe $1,350.

4. *Repeal the Medical-Device Tax.* Obamacare slapped a new 2.3 percent excise tax on medical-device companies' gross sales. Over the next decade, the levy could extract as much as $29 billion from these companies, which make everything from X-ray machines and pacemakers to surgical tools and artificial hips.

   Although the tax is directed at device

firms, patients will foot the bill. According to Richard S. Foster, then chief actuary at the Centers for Medicare and Medicaid Services (CMS), the device tax "would generally be passed through to health consumers in the form of higher drug and device prices and higher insurance premiums." The tax will also yield negative consequences for the economy, as firms will trim their workforces and cut back on investment in research and development.

Already, several device firms – including Stryker, Zimmer, and Welch-Allyn – have announced job cutbacks. Economists at the Manhattan Institute projected that the tax could eliminate 43,000 jobs and more than $3.5 billion in employee compensation.

Benjamin Zycher, an economist and senior fellow at the Pacific Research Institute, estimates that device makers will ratchet down investment in new products by 10 percent over the next seven years. That's equivalent to a $2 billion decrease in R&D spending every year.

Further, the tax applies to gross sales – not profit. So even companies that lose money in a given year will have to fork over cash to the federal government. In March 2013, the Senate approved a nonbinding amendment sponsored by Senators Orrin Hatch (R-Utah) and Amy Klobuchar (D-Minn.) that called for an end to the tax by a margin of 79-20.

5. *Eliminate Bundled Payments.* For starters, Medicare launched a pilot program to develop and evaluate so-called bundled payments as part of an effort to save money. The goal is noble – but the means are not. Under this scheme, doctors and hospitals aren't paid for the services they provide. Instead, they're given a lump sum for each "episode of care," such as a heart attack or a broken bone.

If a health care provider treats its patient for less than the fixed rate, it makes money on the case. But if the treatment costs more than the bundled payment, then the provider has to absorb the difference.

6. *Repeal IPAB.* The law established the Independent Payment Advisory Board, an organization comprising 15 presidential appointees charged with finding ways to reduce spending in Medicare. IPAB is banned from making changes to Medicare's fee-for-service structure or adjusting the level of benefits seniors receive. That leaves one legitimate cost-cutting tool – lowering Medicare's reimbursement rates to health care providers.

However, Medicare's acting chief actuary, Paul Spitalnic, told CMS's chief administrator Marilyn Tavenner that as of April 30, 2013, the projected Medicare five-year per capita growth rate will not exceed the target growth rate – and so there will be no savings target for implementation for 2015.

Reimbursements in Medicare are already low. The program underpaid doctors by

$14.1 billion in 2007. If reimbursements are cut further, many doctors will refuse to treat new program enrollees or will opt out of Medicare entirely.

Indeed, according to a 2012 survey, 52 percent of doctors have limited the access that Medicare patients have to their practice – or they are planning to do so. Given the controversy surrounding the board, it's no wonder that members of Congress from both parties have sponsored legislation scrapping it or that no one had been appointed to it as of April 2013.

7. *Repeal HIT.* In 2014, a new tax on insurance companies goes into effect. There is a bipartisan bill before the House to repeal this tax that will have a negative impact on jobs.

Court Challenges

A handful of court cases will also have a major impact on how Obamacare finally shakes out. Some may make their way to the U.S. Supreme

Court. If successful, there could be dire consequences for the survival of Obamacare.

For starters, nearly 50 lawsuits seek to overturn Obamacare's requirement that employer health plans cover contraception. Brought by the Catholic Church and numerous charities, universities, and religious organizations, the suits allege that the Affordable Care Act's contraception mandate conflicts with their religious teachings and thus violates the First Amendment of the U.S. Constitution. The U.S. Supreme Court may soon be compelled to consider the matter and issue a final judgment.

The Supreme Court has also ordered the Fourth Circuit Court of Appeals in Virginia to move ahead with a suit filed by Liberty University objecting to both the contraception mandate and the mandate requiring employers with 50 or more workers to provide health coverage. If Liberty loses, then its lawyers could immediately appeal.

Oklahoma Attorney General Scott Pruitt is also pursuing a challenge to the employer mandate. Obamacare assesses a financial penalty against employers who do not provide affordable insurance if their employees obtain coverage subsidized by the federal government through the new exchanges. Oklahoma has declined to set up an exchange – and so Pruitt argues that employers in his state should not be subject to the mandate.

The Oklahoma lawsuit also challenges the Affordable Care Act's subsidies. As written, Obamacare dictates that federal subsidies must be distributed through state-based insurance exchanges. Pruitt holds that subsidies therefore can't be distributed through federally run exchanges – like the one that will be established in his state.

2013 is proving to be an action-packed year for Obamacare. But the most disastrous of its provisions will take root in 2014.

The Year Ahead: 2014

Among the most revolutionary provisions are a massive expansion of Medicaid, the joint state and federal health program for low-income Americans and seniors who are disabled or poor; the employer mandate, which orders nearly all firms to furnish coverage to their workers; the individual mandate, which requires nearly all Americans to secure health insurance; and several major regulations that will drive up the cost of insurance for virtually everyone.

Mammoth Medicaid

Obamacare's architects originally envisioned that 32 million Americans would gain insurance coverage thanks to the law. Half of them were to do so through a newly expanded Medicaid program.

First launched in 1965, Medicaid grew quickly. By the time Obamacare became law, the program covered about 60 million people, or 1 in 6 Americans, at a cost of about $427 billion. Medicaid has long been riddled with problems. From 1995 to 2010, Medicaid payments to health care providers steadily declined, such that the program was paying just 92 cents for every dollar of care its beneficiaries consumed, according to a study in the journal *Health Affairs*.

Doctors and hospitals have reacted by either raising prices for patients with private insurance, thereby driving up premiums, or refusing to accept Medicaid patients altogether. Nonetheless, Obamacare's authors decided to expand Medicaid. Total federal and state spending on the program is expected to more than double, from $427 billion in 2010 to $896 billion in 2019.

Starting in 2014, states will have to offer Medicaid to anyone who does not qualify for Medicare and makes less than 133 percent of the poverty line – just over $31,000 a year for a family of four. The federal government will pay for the full cost of the expansion for the first three years and a share that declines on a yearly basis after that, until the federal responsibility reaches 90 percent in 2020. States will be responsible for the rest.

In June 2012, the U.S. Supreme Court

allowed states to opt out of the Medicaid expansion. By May 2013, 25 states had done so or were leaning that way. Twenty-four states and the District of Columbia said that they would participate in Medicaid expansion.

As a result of the Supreme Court's decision, the Congressional Budget Office (CBO) estimated that Medicaid would only cover an additional 12 million people – 6 million less than

---

Thanks to several new rules governing insurance policies, going without coverage will become even more attractive.

---

if the mandated expansion had stood. States that have chosen to go ahead with the Medicaid expansion – among them California, Michigan, Ohio, Illinois, and New Jersey – will sign up newly eligible patients for coverage beginning Jan. 1, 2014.

It's no surprise that many states are choosing not to participate. Even with the promise of federal assistance, the cost to states of expanding the health care entitlement will be crippling. For starters, states must shoulder enormous administrative costs, which could reach nearly $12 billion between 2014 and 2020. Plus, the federal handouts will only cover those who are newly eligible for Medicaid under the Affordable Care Act. States will have to foot the entire bill for those who were eligible for Medicaid before Obamacare but neglected to enroll. That's an estimated 14 million people nationwide.

The New England Journal of Medicine reported the results of a pilot program in Oregon to enroll some low-income adults in Medicaid and then assess the relationship between health outcomes with insurance provided under Medicaid. The findings "showed that Medicaid coverage generated no significant improvements in measured physical health outcomes" compared with not having coverage. These findings do not bode well for those who are expecting to be covered under Obamacare's Medicaid expansion.

Consequently, states could face billions of dollars in new health expenses. In explaining his decision not to expand Texas's Medicaid program, Governor Rick Perry said that the Lone Star State would have faced roughly $27 billion in new costs through 2023.

Some states that have been reluctant to expand Medicaid have asked the Department of Health and Human Services to allow them to use federal money earmarked for expansion of the program to purchase private insurance for low-income people who are new enrollees. Arkansas Governor Mike Beebe has signed such a law. It appears that the administration is prepared to allow Arkansas and a few other states to undertake such an approach. Republican governors in Ohio, Florida, Louisiana, Pennsylvania, and Texas have expressed interest in doing the same.

* * *

Two Mandates

Those who don't get coverage through Medicaid will have to secure it elsewhere. That's thanks to two new mandates – one requiring companies to provide coverage for their workers and the other ordering individuals to obtain insurance.

Both are likely to backfire.

Starting in 2014, employers with 50 or more full-time workers must provide coverage to their full-timers or pay a penalty. That penalty begins at $2,000 per full-time employee, excluding the first 30. For the purposes of the mandate, anyone who works 30 or more hours a week is considered full time. A company is on the hook for the fine if any of its employees receives a tax credit for buying health insurance through the new insurance exchanges.

Just offering health insurance is not enough, though. The plan must also be deemed "affordable" by the federal government. To qualify, plan premiums must cost no more than 9.5

percent of an employee's household income and must cover more than 60 percent of health expenses.

If a firm offers coverage that is not deemed affordable – and if at least one of its employees receives a subsidy through the exchanges – then it will face fines. To determine what it owes, a company will have to perform two calculations. First, it will multiply $3,000 by the number of employees receiving subsidies in the exchanges. Then the firm will have to multiply $2,000 by the number of full-timers in its workforce, minus the first 30 who are exempt. The company's fine is the lesser of those two calculations. The CBO estimates that about a million people per year will be offered coverage deemed "unaffordable" – and that American businesses will face $3 billion in additional taxes each year.

It's not hard to guess how companies will react to these new rules. Businesses just under the 50-employee mark will think twice before hiring additional workers. Many companies will strive to shift employees from full-time to part-time positions or turn staffers into independent contractors.

Walmart announced in late 2012 that it would not offer health insurance to new employees who work fewer than 30 hours a week. It reserved the right to do the same for exist-

---

Insurers are not going to reduce the rates of the elderly so that they're three times what young people currently pay. They're going to hike young adults' premiums.

---

ing workers. Papa John's CEO John Schnatter said that his pizza chain's franchisees would likely cut back employee hours. A New York Applebee's franchisee has said that he may stop hiring because of the additional costs created by the law.

In some cases, both employer and employee may come out ahead if the company cancels the employee's health insurance, pays the fine, and lets the worker take advantage of government subsidies in the exchanges. In 2012, the average annual employer-sponsored individual premium was $5,615, with workers contributing $951, according to the Kaiser Family Foundation. That's substantially more than the fine for ignoring the mandate. So some employers may decide that it makes sense to quit offering coverage altogether.

A 2011 survey of 1,300 companies conducted by the consulting firm McKinsey found that almost a third planned to "definitely or probably" stop providing health coverage by 2014. McKinsey posited that "at least 30 percent" of employers would actually see economic gains from ceasing coverage – and that's even if they provided employees with higher salaries or additional benefits instead of health insurance.

Then there's the individual mandate, which stipulates that Americans must obtain health insurance or pay a fine. That fine starts at $95 or 1 percent of taxable income in 2014, whichever is greater. The next year, the penalty will rise to $325 or 2 percent of income. And in 2016 and thereafter, those who flout the mandate will have to pay the greater of $695 or 2.5 percent of taxable income.

Quite a few folks will do so – 6 million in 2016, according to the CBO. That's because insurance will cost much more than the fine. CBO projects that individual insurance premiums will run about $5,800 annually in 2016, or roughly eight times the standard fine. That's 10 to 13 percent higher than premiums would have been if Obamacare had never become law.

Another 24 million Americans will be exempt from the mandate, among them illegal immigrants, American Indians, parishioners at some churches, and incarcerated people. The regulations also exempt everyone who is technically eligible for Medicaid but lives in a state that has opted out of Obamacare's expansion of the program.

Nearly half a million children have also

been exempted from the requirement to have health insurance, thanks to the complicated rules surrounding the law's definition of *affordability*. Suppose a father's employer offers him individual coverage that costs less than 9.5 percent of his household's income, but a policy that covers his whole family exceeds that figure. In this case, the family is in trouble. It can either pay more than 9.5 percent of its income for family coverage through the employer, or the father can just take the cheaper individual plan, while the kids ignore the mandate without penalty. Subsidized coverage through the exchanges is not an option. This rule will leave about 460,000 kids without access to employer-sponsored coverage.75

The goal of the individual mandate was to expand coverage while also decreasing the cost of insurance. The idea's champions thought that by compelling young, healthy people to pay into the insurance pool, premiums for those who were older and sicker would come down.

But many Americans, particularly young people, will decide that it's in their economic interest to disregard the mandate, forgo coverage, and pay the fine.

Pricier Premiums

Thanks to several new rules governing insurance policies, going without coverage will become even more attractive. Starting in 2014, the principles of "guaranteed issue" and "community rating" will govern the American health insurance market.

Guaranteed issue requires insurers to issue policies to all comers, regardless of health status or family history. Such a reform guarantees that those with pre-existing conditions can get insurance. But it also encourages people to wait until they get sick to purchase coverage. After all, why pay premiums when you're healthy if it's possible to buy a policy after you've landed in the hospital?

The past three years offer a preview of how guaranteed issue will unfold. Back in 2010,

Obamacare required all insurers to guarantee coverage to children. By 2011, 39 states had seen at least one insurer stop offering child-only policies, according to a report by the U.S. Senate Committee on Health, Education, Labor, and Pensions. In 17 states, it became impossible to get a child-only policy. Parents were waiting until their children got sick to buy insurance – and insurers responded by leaving the market.

Consequently, 22 states and the District of Columbia had to take legislative or regulatory action to try to expand the availability of child-only policies. Despite those efforts, insurers still didn't offer child-only coverage by May 2012 in three of the states.

Community rating restricts what insurers can charge. Starting in 2014, insurers will be banned from charging elderly customers more than three times what they charge young people. The feds will also limit the degree to which insurance companies can adjust premiums based on family composition, tobacco usage, and geography.

But older folks use more health care than do younger ones. Americans ages 45 to 64 years spent, on average, $5,511 on health care in 2009, according to the Kaiser Family Foundation. For Americans ages 18 to 24, that number was only $1,834. For 25- to 44-year-olds, it was $2,739. Insurers are not going to reduce the rates of the elderly so that they're three times what young people currently pay. They're going to hike young adults' premiums.

Indeed, community rating will engender a 190 percent rate increase for younger, healthier people living in Milwaukee, according to a survey of five cities conducted by the American Action Forum. Across all five cities, the average premiums for young people will rise 169 percent.

Eighty percent of adults below the age of 30 will pay more for insurance – even after taking subsidies available through the exchanges into account. A third of those between the ages of 30 and 44 will similarly face premium hikes.

Yet another factor exerting upward pressure

on premiums will be the "essential health benefit" (EHB) rules. All individual and small-group plans must cover government-mandated benefits beginning in 2014. The rules cover 10 categories of care, including not only emergencies and hospitalizations but also maternity care, substance-abuse services, and children's dental and vision care.

Plans are divided into four groups: platinum, gold, silver, and bronze. Plans with these designations must cover 90, 80, 70, and 60 percent of patients' health costs, respectively. More generous plans will have lower deductibles and higher premiums. The new rules also limit deductibles in the small-group market to $2,000 for individuals and $4,000 for families.

Such a generous definition of *essential* drives up the cost of health insurance. Many citizens would happily forgo coverage of services they don't expect to need in exchange for lower premiums. A 25-year-old single man, for instance, doesn't have much use for maternity care. Nor does a teetotaler for alcohol-addiction treatment. Obamacare doesn't allow for such variations in demand and instead imposes high-priced, one-size-fits-all insurance.

Further, high-deductible plans have proved to be an effective way of keeping health spending down—particularly when coupled with tax-advantaged health savings accounts (HSAS).

When high-deductible, consumer-directed health plans became widespread in the mid-2000s, the growth rate of health care costs slowed. In a report earlier this year, the RAND Corporation found that if such health plans grew to compose half of all employee-provided insurance, costs would drop by $57 billion a year.

Obamacare also directly increases the price of insurance by levying a new health insurance tax (HIT) in 2014. This "fee," as it's called in the law, will be assessed on health insurers based on their market share. The feds expect to raise $8 billion from the new tax in 2014. It climbs to $11.3 billion in 2015 and 2016, to $13.9 billion in 2017, and to $14.3 billion thereafter. The Joint Committee on

> *The next president will have the chance to repeal Obamacare and replace it with real health care reform.*

Taxation estimates that the tax will exceed $100 billion over the next 10 years.

And while insurers will write the checks to the federal Treasury, the tax will be "largely passed through to consumers in the form of higher premiums," according to the CBO.

A 2011 analysis conducted by Oliver Wyman, a consultancy, estimated that the health insurance tax would increase premiums by 1.9 percent to 2.3 percent in 2014. Individuals would see an average increase in premiums of $2,150 over 10 years; the average rise in premiums for a family plan would total $5,080 over the same period.

All told, the Society of Actuaries projects that monthly nongroup per-member health costs will increase by nearly a third under Obamacare. In some states, costs could rise 80 percent.

In spite of the multibillion-dollar expansion of Medicaid, the employer mandate, and the individual mandate, the federal government estimates that nearly 10 percent of Americans – or 30 million people – will still be uninsured in 2016 after Obamacare is fully in place. Yet the law ensures that businesses, government, and individuals will all pay more for health care – if they can afford it at all.

That's not the health care solution Americans have been searching for. It's time for health reform that will truly expand access to care and reduce costs. It's time for a cure for Obamacare.

The Replacement Plan

The House has voted to repeal Obamacare more than 30 times. But its efforts have gone nowhere, as President Obama cannot be expected to repeal his signature piece of legislation.

Once he leaves the White House, the repeal movement must gain momentum. If repeal comes about, our leaders must have a replacement agenda ready – one that will truly expand access to health care and lower costs. Here's what should be on it.

1. *Change the federal tax code.* Congress must grant individuals the ability to purchase health insurance with pretax dollars – just as businesses can.

    Our present tax regime encourages Americans to get health coverage through work – coverage whose full cost they don't realize. Consequently, patients have an incentive to overconsume care. That drives up costs for the entire health care system. Further, with equal tax treatment, Americans could select coverage that suits their needs and budget rather than their employer's.

    To make coverage more affordable for

individuals who don't get coverage through work, Congress could institute a refundable tax credit to help offset the cost of insurance.

2. *Expand the availability of health savings accounts.* Patients can save pretax dollars for health services. Doing so would encourage Americans to shop smartly for their care, as they'd be spending their own money. It would also lead to transparency in health care pricing – a laudable goal.

3. *Allow purchase of insurance across state lines.* There's no reason that insurance policies issued in Rhode Island should cost 2.5 times what they do in Alabama. Freeing the national insurance market would do wonders to foment competition and thereby lower costs.

4. *Expand high-risk pools.* For those who cannot find affordable coverage because of pre-existing conditions, the feds should seed a

robust network of high-risk pools at the state level. Such pools were functioning well in many states before Obamacare – delivering coverage to those who needed it without raising premiums for everyone else. Congressman Joe Pitts (R-Pa.) introduced a bill in April 2013 that, if passed, would have taken $4 billion from the Prevention and Public Health Fund to reinstate funding to the temporary high-risk pools. However, the bill was pulled before it went to a vote.

5. *Eliminate EHR mandate.* Another way to reduce the cost of medical care: Scrap the expensive mandates forcing doctors and hospitals to set up electronic health records. The average initial cost of an electronic health records (EHR) system is $44,000 per physician, with ongoing maintenance estimated at $8,500 a year. Those costs are passed directly to patients.

6. *Eliminate EHB mandate.* Slashing another set of mandates – those requiring all policies

to cover certain benefits – would do even more to reduce health care costs. Benefit mandates can raise the cost of a standard insurance policy anywhere from 10 to 50 percent, depending on the state, the number of mandates, and the type of policy.

7. *Medical malpractice reform.* States should also reform their medical-malpractice laws. Each year, more than $100 billion in health care expenditures is driven by concerns from health care providers about medical liability. Bringing some common sense to our malpractice system would reduce those wasteful expenditures – and usher in lower costs for patients.

8. *Reform Medicare and Medicaid.* In addition, our leaders must rein in out-of-control spending on entitlements, specifically Medicaid and Medicare. Right now, the feds effectively encourage states to expand Medicaid by kicking in from $1 to $3.25 for every dollar a state spends on the program.

We can't afford that. To limit cost growth, Congress should distribute block grants to each state. In so doing, lawmakers would encourage – if not order – states to manage their Medicaid programs wisely. Alternatively, Congress could permit states to privatize their Medicaid programs.

Spending on Medicare, meanwhile, is north of $550 billion. It's projected to climb above $1 trillion by 2022. That's not sustainable. The solution? Reserve Medicare for those who truly need it – the poor and the aged.

American life expectancy has grown by eight years since Medicare was established in 1965. Consequently, the eligibility age for Medicare should increase too. Further, federal officials should furnish seniors with means-tested vouchers to purchase privately administered coverage. By empowering seniors to take charge of their own care, such a system would stoke competition among insurers and health care providers who are eager for seniors' business – and would thereby lower costs.

9. *Support Medical Tourism.* Finally, there's one way that Americans can reduce health costs on their own, with no congressional action necessary – by considering medical tourism. Nearly 550 top-notch medical facilities across the world have been certified by the Joint Commission International, an accreditation organization.

The medical-tourism group Patients Beyond Borders estimates that Americans can save 25 to 40 percent on their medical bills by traveling to Brazil. For Costa Rica, it's 45 to 60 percent. And in Thailand, the savings can reach 70 percent.

Solutions like these will put America on the path to addressing its health-cost crisis and ensuring that quality care is available to all. Universal choice is the key to universal coverage.

The Cure for Obamacare

The next president will have the chance to repeal Obamacare and replace it with real health care reform. But what if he or she does not follow through?

That's a frightening thought. Obamacare threatens to turn our world-class health care system into one resembling the bureaucratic

---

Obamacare threatens to turn our world-class health care system into one resembling the bureaucratic monstrosities in place in countries like Great Britain and Canada.

---

monstrosities in place in countries like Great Britain and Canada.

The Affordable Care Act's first casualty will be our nation's finances. According to CMS, health spending will rise by 7.4 percent and account for 18.2 percent of GDP by 2014. By

2050, health care could consume 40 percent of our economy.

Between 2015 and 2021, CMS estimates that health spending will grow at a 6.2 percent annual clip. Expenditures by Medicare are expected to grow 6.7 percent per year, on average, from 2014 to 2021.

Premiums are sure to go up too. Since the president took office, family health insurance premiums have risen by an average of $3,065. In 2014, private insurance premiums should increase 7.9 percent. For the following seven years, they'll grow by 5.9 percent a year.

By and large, Obamacare's supporters don't dispute these projections. But they don't believe that Obamacare is to blame for run-away cost growth. In fact, they believe that Obamacare didn't go far enough – and that outright government control of the health care marketplace is the only way to solve the cost crisis.

Indeed, prominent liberal observers, such as Ezra Klein of *The Washington Post*, have wondered why congressional Democrats have avoided pushing for a government-run public insurance option since Obamacare took effect.

Perhaps liberal lawmakers don't think that a public option is enough. Legislation proposing a single-payer, government-run health care system has been offered in every Congress since 2003. President Obama himself said in 2003, "I happen to be a proponent of a single-payer universal health care program."

As Obamacare's cost-inflating consequences manifest themselves in the coming years, the push for a single-payer "Medicare for All" program will likely grow. This is a dangerous prospect. Similar government-run health care schemes have not only failed to rein in costs or deliver quality care everywhere they've been tried, but they've also proved impossible to get rid of, even after their failures have become apparent.

Canada's system of government-run medicine is one I know all too well, as an ex-Canadian.

Canada's march to single-payer began in 1946,

when Saskatchewan instituted government-funded hospital insurance. The federal government followed suit in 1957, funding hospital insurance for the entire country.

In 1961, Saskatchewan became the first province to fund full medical insurance for all its residents. By 1966, the Canadian government had provided money to provinces that followed Saskatchewan's lead. Two years later, they all did.

Canada spends 11.4 percent of its GDP on health care – substantially less than the United States does. But the Canadian system has kept costs down through price controls. And as Canadians know firsthand, price controls lead to shortages and rationing.

In 2012, Canadian patients waited 8.5 weeks for a consultation with a specialist after receiving a referral from their primary-care doctor, according to the Fraser Institute. Once they actually saw a specialist, they waited another 9.3 weeks for treatment. Members of my own family have borne the deadly consequences of Canada's rationing. In June 2005, my mother thought that she might have colon cancer. But her primary-care doctor ruled out that possibility after giving her an X-ray. When she asked about a colonoscopy, she was told that she was too old. There were too many younger people with serious symptoms who were already on a waiting list for the test.

By early December, my mother was experiencing symptoms related to colon cancer. She was taken to the hospital in an ambulance. She received her colonoscopy then, all right, but passed away two weeks later from metastasized colon cancer.

Or take the case of my uncle. In 1999, he was diagnosed with non-Hodgkin's lymphoma. At the time, a new drug called Rituxan had shown enormous success in fighting the disease. But it wasn't on the formulary in British Columbia, Canada, so it was unavailable to my uncle. Had he lived in America, he might have survived.

When the government pays for health care, saving money is more important than saving lives. Bureaucrats have an incentive to delay –

or deny – the introduction of new, costly drugs. Indeed, less than a quarter of new drugs certified as safe and effective by Canadian regulators between 2004 and 2010 had become eligible for reimbursement under the provinces' public drug programs as of January 2012.

Canadians also lack access to other advanced medical technologies. Canada has 34 percent fewer MRI machines per million residents than the average developed country does, according to the Organisation for Economic Co-operation and Development (OECD). And it has 37 percent fewer CT scanners per million people than the average among its OECD peers.

Shortcomings like these contribute to Canada's poor health outcomes. Five-year survival rates for breast cancer, colorectal cancer, and prostate cancer are higher in the United States than in my home country. Britain's government-run health care system, the National Health Service, is equally dysfunctional. It offers a preview of how some of

Obamacare's strategies for trimming health costs could play out.

Obamacare's Patient-Centered Outcomes Research Institute, for instance, is modeled after Britain's notorious rationing board, the National Institutes for Health and Clinical Excellence (NICE). NICE regularly captures headlines for denying sick patients everything from Alzheimer's medication to cancer treatments because they're not "cost-effective" – even if they're proven to keep people alive.

Not surprisingly, health outcomes for Brit-

When the government pays for health care, saving money is more important than saving lives.

ish patients are quite bleak. A study published this year found that British patients with late-stage breast cancer have lower rates of survival than their peers in five other developed countries, including Sweden and Canada.

The *British Journal of Medicine* recently reported that, relative to other countries, from 1990 to 2010, "UK performance worsened on most measures of healthy life expectancy."

Countries like Britain and Canada – with their long wait times; reduced access or even outright denial of the best medical care; and worse health outcomes – offer a preview of what's ahead for the United States if the Affordable Care Act remains the law of the land.

The only question is whether the American people will turn against that future – and close the book on Obamacare. If not, we will be on the road to serfdom, and there will be no off-ramp.

First American edition published in 2013 by Encounter Books,
an activity of Encounter for Culture and Education, Inc.,
a nonprofit, tax exempt corporation.
Encounter Books website address: www.encounterbooks.com

Manufactured in the United States and printed on
acid-free paper. The paper used in this publication meets
the minimum requirements of ansi/niso z39.48 1992
(R 1997) (*Permanence of Paper*).

FIRST AMERICAN EDITION

LIBRARY OF CONGRESS CATALOGING-IN-PUBLICATION DATA

Pipes, Sally, 1945–
The cure for Obamacare / Sally C. Pipes.
pages   cm. -- (Encounter broadsides)
ISBN 978-1-59403-714-6 (pbk. : alk. paper)
ISBN 978-1-59403-715-3 (ebook)
1. Health insurance policies—United States.
2. Health care reform—United States.
3. Medical policy—United States.   I. Title.
HG9384.5.P57   2013
368.4′200973—dc23
2013019141

10 9 8 7 6 5 4 3 2 1